Secrets of the World's Contrarian Investors

by Leo Gough

Contents

Contents

– Chapter One –

What makes a contrarian investor?

Contrarianism is a cast of mind rather than a formal theory; most, if not all, of the greatest investors can be described as 'contrarian' despite their widely differing expertise, methods and philosophies. What gives a diffident, calculating prodigy (Warren Buffet), a high-born gambler (James Goldsmith) and a committed Christian who prays before important meetings (John Templeton) something in common is their determination as individuals to make their own decisions regardless of what the majority of investors are doing.

For contrarianism is not merely doing the opposite of what the crowd is doing, since sometimes the crowd is right – for a time. Contrarianism really means developing your own approach to investing and working for the long haul. Thus, while their methods may be different from one another, contrarians do not regard opinions as ideas to be followed blindly, whether they are popular or are the consensus of some professional group such as stock market analysts. They are acutely aware that short-term movements in the market are moved by 'investor psychology', that is, by the way the majority happens to be thinking at the moment.

To understand how this works in practice, let's think of a contrarian investor as a seasoned traveller taking a flight, and examine the comparison in some detail:

Travelling by aeroplane was once a luxury that few could afford; now, half a century after the commercialisation of airlines, there are few people who haven't travelled on a plane, and, indeed, the majority do so once every two years, at least. Airline travel has become a mundane activity – everyone knows what to expect, and how, in general terms, it works. The same is true of the Stock Market, although on a smaller scale – technical developments and the growth of the number of equity investors both in the UK and abroad has vastly increased the amount of information available about companies as well as about the markets. In both cases, you would expect people to behave rationally in what is a familiar situation.

But if you were a seasoned traveller observing what happens inside the cabin when a passenger plane lands at its destination, you might think otherwise. Invariably, as soon as the plane has come to a halt, everyone leaps out of their seats and incompetently tries to collect their luggage from the overhead lockers, causing chaos in the process. Our traveller sits patiently in his seat, knowing that the buses have not yet arrived to take the passengers to the terminal. Minutes pass – sometimes half an hour – until the buses have arrived, the gangway is in situ, and the cabin staff open the doors. The traveller calmly takes his bags while the other passengers rush for the door. He makes it off the plane with the stragglers, those too old or infirm to have forced their way to the front earlier. As he walks down the gangway he scans the buses – are they likely all to leave together (which is usual), or will one leave before another? The traveller picks a bus and gets in – everyone else is already inside, so he is right by the door. When the bus arrives at the terminal, the traveller is the first one off.

Our traveller is like a contrarian investor. The plane trip is a fixed system over which he has little control (far less, arguably, than in the Stock Market), but he can take a few steps to maximise his comfort, minimise his expenditure of energy, and give himself the best possible chance of getting out of the airport quickly. Simply by learning how the system works and acting accordingly, he outperforms the majority who, although they ought to know better, do the obvious, but stupid, thing.

Human beings are social animals, and whether they are in an airport or contemplating their investments they tend to make herd-following decisions, especially during times of stress. Many financial institutions exploit this by selling the wrong sort of pension and mortgage, offering poor rates of return and so on. This can only work if customers feel impelled to act without either taking the time to learn the rules or to consider their options carefully.

It is not only the public who fail to take the long view, either; analysts, economists, fund managers, bankers, brokers – in fact, most financial 'insiders' – all have a tendency to do what they see that their colleagues are doing. It is not their money, after all, and keeping their jobs is more important to them than performing well.

Contrarians don't usually entrust their money to others for precisely this reason; it is likely to go into 'popular' investments, and when the popularity fades, so does the asset value. Looking after your own money, if you have the time and inclination to do so, ought to produce better results than by leaving it to others. At least, this is the attitude of the contrarian; if in practice you find that you cannot outperform the indices, perhaps you should put your money in an index tracker fund.

Once the traveller is through the passport control, he strolls down to baggage collection, checking which conveyor belt is scheduled for his flight, he knows he has some minutes to spare. He also observes that he is among the first to arrive in the baggage area. Time to go to the Gents' – the best time, since there is no rush, as there always is on the plane. He is in the Third World, so the Gents' in the baggage collection is out of order, and looks as if it has been so for several years. No matter. The traveller saunters back to the conveyor belt, collects a trolley, and picks a point near to the hole out of which the bags will come. He wonders why other people don't do this – most of them situate themselves near the middle of the conveyor belt, presumably because this gives them the sensual delight of seeing their luggage move slowly towards them.

A long delay follows. All the passengers have now arrived. Their earlier attempts to hurry have in no way affected the outcome – everyone is now stuck waiting for their baggage, just as they were all stuck on the plane waiting for the buses.

Efforts in investing are frequently like this – frantic comparisons of performance figures and agonising over what to buy or to sell do not, on their own, produce a good return. Contrarians are well aware of the actuaries' dictum that, in the very long-term, you can expect an inflation-adjusted annual return of between 2% and 4%. At such rates you can expect your money to double in real terms in between 18 and 36 years, which, while hardly exciting, is much better than seeing your savings diminish. While outstanding investors have achieved much higher returns over several decades, even the astonishing Warren Buffet, who started with a few thousand dollars and is now worth 10 billion dollars, has 'only' achieved a real return of 28% annually (for Berkshire Hathaway 1970-1994).

Back at the airport it is time for the baggage lottery. Some intelligent souls think that if you check in your luggage as late as you can, it will be the first off the plane, but experience teaches otherwise – there are other factors involved, principally the way in which the hold was loaded and unloaded (which we cannot know).

The conveyor belt starts to move, and bags appear. They travel all the way round the belt without being claimed and disappear through the exit hole. After some time, the traveller sees his bag, swings it with one deft movement on to his trolley, and within minutes is outside, boarding a bus to his destination. He is not the first to get out, but, unless by chance his bag is amongst the last to be unloaded, he is unlikely to be among the last.

There are points (such as the choice of bus) where he must make a decision and live with it if he is wrong, but in general he is playing for a gain in time of, say, twenty minutes. Everyone else will get out of the airport (assuming that their luggage has not been lost and that their passports are in order) at about the same time.

All this may seem like not much reward for a lot of effort, but if our contrarian takes a flight every day, he will significantly increase his chances of getting out of the airport early, simply by observing the actions of those around him and taking action. As with investment, consistency of effort produces a better result. And better results produce yet better results through the power of compound interest.

The most important feature of consistency is the most obvious one; if you are investing in equities now, are you not likely to be doing so for the rest of your life? There is ample evidence to show that by keeping at least part of your funds invested at all times you are likely to do better than if you frequently move your money in and out of investment classes. And if you are doing it for life, should you not plan accordingly, and think it out from first principles?

Contrarians are in the Stock Market for the long haul, even if they do not hold particular shares for very long. This is deeply contrarian behaviour – most people simply do not do this, just as they do not usually do anything consistently enough, and for long enough, to achieve outstanding results. In other words, most people are perpetually changing their goals and opinions.

Opinion is the occupational disease of investment. We are flooded with opinions, many of which are dishonest or silly, in professional journals as well as in the mass media. Share prices go up and down precisely because of investors' opinions about what the future holds in store for the companies concerned. For many investors, even sophisticated ones, reality is the same as the current consensus, which is always changing.

Contrarians learn to ignore opinions, or to read between the lines. To do this, they need to develop their own individual methods. In the next chapter, we will look at some ways in which this is done.

– Chapter Two –

Contrarian approaches

Given that you are investing for the rest of your life, you will need some way of measuring your performance. Week-on-week figures might be appropriate for a shop, or for a professional share trader who lives on quick, small profits, but the long-term investor needs to take a longer time-span. Comparing returns year-on-year is more useful, but only if you refuse to be influenced by bad years. We know that there are bull and bear market cycles, and that there will be lean periods as well as plentiful ones, so we can expect our performance to reflect this. Judging your performance in five-year chunks is more likely to reflect your real performance through the cycles of boom and bust.

Stock Market investing is a remarkably private activity. Unless you are very big indeed, or you want publicity, there is no reason, for anyone to know how you have performed. For this reason most of the individuals who are known to be outstandingly successful investors run funds where their progress is publicly monitored. They are also old – to judge someone else's performance you need plenty of years' worth of activity to examine, so it makes sense to study people who have been in the markets for several decades. As we will see overleaf, this has the drawback that what worked for, say, Warren Buffett in the

1950s may not work today. This doesn't invalidate the effort, however. Although circumstances may be different, the impossibility of predicting the future remains constant, so we can learn something from how such people made their judgements at the time.

Contrarians must be realistic about this. The future is unpredictable. If I buy a share today, I cannot know what its price will be next week, or in a year's time, or in ten years' time. I can look back at what I have done in the past and if I remember the reasons for my decisions I may be able to learn something, but this can never give me a cast-iron certainty about the future. If my performance has remained consistently good throughout a series of different conditions, it can give me some confidence that my methods have been good, but that is all. Likewise, studying the history of a share price does not tell me its future.

So if it is not possible to predict the future, what are these outstanding investors up to? Quite simply, they are making judgements. How they come to their judgements is unique to them, and is as dependent on their personal make-up as it is on their expertise.

Warren Buffett

Warren Buffett is a good example of this. Here is a man who is socially isolated and brilliantly quick at mental calculations – in short, a nerd. He has lived in the same modest house in Omaha, Nebraska since 1957, drank several cans of Pepsi Cola a day until he switched to Cherry Coke, and spends most of his life compulsively studying company reports. His knowledge is encyclopaedic – it is said that in his early twenties he was familiar with the financial details of all US quoted companies. His success is legendary. As his funds grew, he began concentrating on large holdings in a few companies, flying in the face of the conventional advice to diversify, and becoming the archetypal 'lumpy' portfolio holder. No doubt he would change tactics again if he thought the circumstances warranted it.

Although not cut out for a managerial role, Buffett is fascinated by business. Unlike his mentor, Benjamin Graham, who restricted himself to objective mathematical techniques for stock-picking, Buffett is a believer. He has his own ideas of the types of business that do well, and has been known to monitor a company for years before investing in it. He says that there are only a very few really good businesses, and that they have the following characteristics:

- They have a good Return on Capital Expended and low gearing.

- Buffett can understand what they do.

- The managers have due regard for their shareholders.

- They are unlikely to suffer from state interference.

- They profit from growth elsewhere (e.g. TV companies, newspapers).

- Their stock is low and their stock turnover is high.

- They have predictable earnings.

- They have good cash flow.

- They have a franchise. This means that they are companies that are so dominant in their market that they have great freedom in setting prices and are unlikely to suffer from competition (e.g. Amex, Coca Cola).

Thus, Buffett combines fundamental analysis with value judgements about the nature and prospects of individual companies. He does not seem to be very interested in the macro-economic views so beloved by economists employed by financial institutions. This is not, in itself, remarkable, but what makes it so is that Buffett is an unusually honest man and expects the same of others. There is no double-think in his mind, no mealy-mouthed pronunciamentos about the state of the market – just a total intellectual dedication to investment based on an upright, moral view of the world. In short, Buffett has made investment virtues of his own natural tendencies.

James Goldsmith

Making a virtue of what you already are is almost the only thing Buffett has in common with the late billionaire Sir James Goldsmith. Goldsmith spent his early years at the Carlton Hotel at Cannes, one of the many luxury hotels run by his father, a former British MP.

Goldsmith's own performance in the 1997 general election may have been comical, but this reflects the man. Mavericks make good businessmen and bad politicians.

While Buffett has spent his life hiding in Nebraska, Goldsmith lived at the centre of a whirlwind. Eloping with an heiress as a youth, he hit the headlines for the first time. His young wife tragically died in childbirth, and Goldsmith became embroiled in a highly public battle over his child, culminating in a court case in Paris in which a member of the Spanish royal family was ordered to hand over the child to him. With fatherhood came working for a living, and Goldsmith started in a small way, selling medical products in France. His private life has been glamorously unconventional – he openly maintained wives and mistresses at the same time. He was a close friend of Lord Lucan, who disappeared following a murder, and was a celebrated libel litigant.

Just another upper-class yobbo parasiting the productive sections of society? Not exactly. Firstly, he made his own money; he did not come into a large inheritance. Secondly, he was a master of company predation, which cannot be achieved by nepotism.

Goldsmith did not have the massive intellect of Buffett, but he does know his business well. He has used his entrée into society to good effect, and basked in his larger-than-life reputation. As an investor, we can regard him as a specialist in acquisitions, embarking on a succession of highly lucrative takeovers and takeover attempts during the 1980s.

In 1979 Sir James Goldsmith controlled Cavenham Foods, an international conglomerate in food manufacturing and retailing. Deciding to concentrate on retailing, Goldsmith sold off his manufacturing interests piecemeal, raising £100 million by early 1980.

He began to buy shares in Diamond International, a US wood products conglomerate with sales of $1.2 billion, but which had low profits. Discovering that Diamond owned, since the 19th century, 1.6 million acres of land which was valued at only £27 million pounds, Goldsmith announced publicly that he planned to make a bid for the company. Meanwhile, Diamond launched a bid for another wood products company, Brooks Scanlon, to be financed by a new issue of Diamond shares.

Goldsmith then offered Diamond shareholders $45 per share on the condition that they rejected the Brooks Scanlon deal, or $40 if it was concluded, and increased his own holding in Diamond to 6%. The Stock Market price of Diamond's shares was $32.65, but it increased to $38.20 after Goldsmith's announcement.

Goldsmith then tried, and failed, to obtain an injunction to prevent Diamond from holding its AGM. At the AGM, however, the main shareholders in Diamond were divided in their support, so the smaller investors would have to be given a vote on whether or not to accept the bid.

Diamond made a deal with Goldsmith that they would allow him to increase his stake to 25% on the condition that Goldsmith would not raise it above 40%, and also gave him the right to appoint three directors to the board.

Diamond's shares had gone up to $50 in the market, but on the news of this latest agreement they dropped to $38.25. Goldsmith obtained 21.5 million shares, but the merger with Brook Scanlon went ahead, so he owned only 24% of the merged company; the purchase cost him $105 million.

During the following year a recession hit the wood products industry. Although Diamond was able to maintain its turnover at $1.28 billion, its profits were only $41 million, and the share price dropped to $29.

The ex-boss of Brooks Scanlon, who now owned 1.6 million Diamond shares, approached Goldsmith, offering to sell the shares at $42 (a premium of $13 per share over the current market price). Goldsmith bought them, increasing his holding in Diamond to about 40%; Diamond's management caved in, and sold Goldsmith a controlling interest in the company.

Goldsmith now borrowed the vast sum of $660 million to purchase the rest of Diamond and inject cash into the company. The interest rate was as high as 18%, and Diamond's profits would barely cover a third of the annual interest payments on the loan.

Goldsmith then proceeded to sell off some of Diamond's subsidiaries, paying off, by 1983, all of his debt. This sell-off stimulated adverse criticism of him as an asset-stripper.

Goldsmith concentrated on Diamond's vast holdings of forest land, cutting costs and building new saw mills to increase productivity. The Stock Market went up, and by the summer of 1983 his forests were valued at $723 million, representing a net profit to Goldsmith of around $500 million.

The US's Reagan administration had taken wide measures to deregulate the economy, and a craze for mergers began, driving up the prices of listed companies. Goldsmith continued a highly successful policy of acquisitions.

In December 1984, Goldsmith announced his intention of buying 15-20% of Crown Zellerbach, another conglomerate with 2 million acres of cheap forest and large oil holdings; its shares were then at $28. Three months later, he had invested about $80 million to purchase 8.6% of the company's shares, which by then stood at $33.25.

The 'merger-mania' of the 1980s was in full swing, and boards everywhere were struggling to make their companies look as unattractive as possible to potential bidders. The method they used most was the 'poison pill'; an arrangement to issue new shares at a large discount to existing shareholders in the event of a bid, which has the effect of making a company too expensive for a bidder to buy.

Crown Zellerbach had a 'poison pill' which became effective if someone bought 20% of the company's shares. After an abortive attempt to find another buyer, it approached Goldsmith to offer a deal by which he would acquire no more than 19.5% of the company for the next three years, and Crown would cancel the poison pill. Goldsmith made a counteroffer which was rejected; he then proceeded to purchase shares to give him a total of 19.6% of the company, just below the trigger level of the poison pill. Crown was now under pressure – once Goldsmith triggered the poison pill, Crown would become prohibitively expensive to other bidders.

Following bitter litigation, Goldsmith managed to acquire a controlling interest in the company, and it was split into two, the forests and oil going to Goldsmith, and the rest going to a paper company. For $550 million, Goldsmith had acquired assets which were now estimated to be worth about $990 million.

Clearly you need access to large amounts of money in order to buy companies, but this does not mean that lesser mortals have nothing to learn from Goldsmith; anyone can specialise in mergers and acquisitions in a small way, hanging on to the coat tails of the predators, so to speak, by moving in and out of shares in the relevant companies.

The biggest coup of all

In 1986 Goldsmith tried to take over the Goodyear corporation, but failed after a public outcry against the bid, accepting a profit of $93 million for himself and his financial backers. He considered making other bids, but eventually decided that the market was overvalued and that there were no more bargains to be had. By selling his entire shareholdings in early 1987, Goldsmith pulled off the biggest coup of his whole career – shortly afterwards the world's Stock Markets crashed on Black Monday, dropping further than they had for nearly sixty years, and wiping billions off the market value of companies across the globe.

Spotting the peak of a bull market

At the time of writing, it appears that by any sensible measure, both London and Wall Street are grossly overvalued. This inevitably begs the question of how one should behave and encourages people to chatter to one another about their prognostications.

An actuary told me the other day that he had been repeating dire warnings about the market to his bosses for the last four years. Recently a German banker remarked to me that if you regard the 1987 crash as a correction, then there has been a bull market for some 20 years, the longest ever. A rich friend tells me that she has sold all her equities.

Perhaps the most telling sign of all is that my friend Conrad, an impoverished Oxbridge dropout, who spent part of the 1970s in a Spanish prison and is now a computer programmer, is hot – desperate, in fact – to buy his first shares. When the idea that you can make money in the Stock Market reaches people like Conrad, perhaps share enthusiasm has reached its high-tide mark. In Conrad we have the classic punter who wants to buy for all the wrong reasons and has no expertise in evaluating the shares on offer.

Yet the market may keep on going. No one knows when prices will adjust to reflect underlying values, or even if they ever will. Certainly the successful investors discussed above do not. While Goldsmith may have got out just before Black Monday, this seems to have been more from a life decision to retire from business than any desire to re-enter later. Buffet wound up what was then his main fund in 1969 during a bull market saying that:

"I am out of step with present conditions... I will not abandon a previous approach whose logic I understand... even though it may mean forgoing large and apparently easy profits..."

So if you think that the bull market is reaching its peak, you might resist from buying if you can't find good value among companies, but there is no necessity to sell good long-term holdings if you plan to continue holding them for the long-term. Good businesses will go on earning profits and paying dividends far into the future, in spite of stock market fluctuations.

John Templeton

Born in humble circumstances in Tennessee, Sir John Templeton was a scholarship student at Yale before going on to be a Rhodes scholar at Oxford in the 1930s. At the outbreak of World War II he borrowed $10,000 and bought some 100 different US shares with it, all of them 'dogs' selling at less than $1 per share. His reasoning was that the war would boost America's fortunes and that the companies which were currently the least wanted were the ones most likely to perform well.

This scatter-gun approach worked. By the end of the war his portfolio had increased in value by some 400%, providing him with the money to set up as a fund manager. Templeton ran the business for many years before selling it and moving to the Bahamas for a kind of early retirement. He took with him one small fund to manage, which by the late Seventies had multiplied twenty times in twenty years, and his reputation was made.

Unlike the narrow and deep specialisations of Buffett and Goldsmith, Templeton made a point of entering a wide number of foreign Stock Markets long before it became fashionable for fund managers to do so. Living in the Bahamas brought him into contact with foreign captains of industry, providing him with an international perspective that most of the English-speaking world lacks.

Although he has now retired, Templeton's fund is still run according to his principles; one interesting point about its internationalism is that it virtually ignores exchange rate prognostications – in fact, it has no department for forecasting the fluctuations of foreign currencies. This is deeply contrarian; the conventional wisdom is that the danger of devaluation greatly outweighs the chance of profits in foreign markets and that, therefore, it is more important to watch the country and its currency than it is to watch the companies that reside within their borders. The Templeton fund argues that if you have selected the companies properly, the companies themselves will take steps to protect their value in hard currency terms.

Templeton has been a great diversifier and a bargain hunter who sought out little-known companies across the world. Like Buffett he worries about the dangers of state interference, and with more reason, since he has invested in many less than stable regimes.

Perhaps his most famous coup was to have invested in Japan early and to have got out early, long before its notorious crash. This, say the fund's current managers, was decided upon on the basis of the changes in values of the individual equities it held, rather than on some god-like assessment of the 'country risk'. Indeed, the fund has an aversion to 'big decisions' of the "We'll put 30% of our money into Brazil" kind; the focus is always on the values of the companies themselves primarily, with local political and regulatory factors analysed in terms of how they affect investments. All common sense, you might think, but it is the kind of common sense that is unlearned by corporate types during their training.

Templeton has published the following investment maxims:

- Invest for real returns.

- Keep an open mind.

- Never follow the crowd.

- Everything changes.

- Avoid the popular.

- Learn from your mistakes.

- Buy during times of pessimism.

- Hunt for value and bargains.

- Search worldwide.

- No-one knows everything.

These are entirely unobjectionable contrarian notions, but they are not necessarily easy to put into practice. The really exceptional precept is to 'search worldwide'; very few people really do this. To be truly familiar with the rules, accounting procedures and other realities of obscure stock exchanges – which are invariably different from London and Wall Street – takes years of effort. To see how a trader approaches these matters it is worth reading Jim Rogers' *Investment Biker*, in which this undoubtedly successful investor reveals a hilarious ignorance of other cultures.

Whether private investors can afford the time and effort necessary to familiarise themselves with the smaller foreign markets is moot – most would reject the notion out of hand – yet it seems to me that merely to concentrate on UK shares could be short-sighted. All countries have a vested interest in discouraging their citizens from exporting their capital, whether or not this is admitted, and there are many subtle obstacles to investing in foreign markets.

This is clearly an area in which specialisation could pay off. There is also the spectre of the demise of five hundred years of Western World dominance to consider, not that it is likely to happen overnight, but that it may be that we see Asia asserting itself increasingly in world affairs in the future. The rapid development of the Pacific Rim nations is extraordinary – 'Go East, young man', would seem to be the right advice to the ambitious.

Bargain hunting

Bargain hunting is another notion which sounds good but is difficult to put into practice. First, it takes a great deal of effort. It is argued that Benjamin Graham's strict value investing criteria, as set out in *Security Analysis* (1944 Graham and Dodd) will not currently produce a single UK candidate for investment – hence the need to look overseas.

Private investors as a rule do not understand how to interpret company accounts, which is the first essential. If you have not learned to do so already, it is worth the effort! The great conceptual barrier to the neophyte is the assumption that there is one straightforward method of accounting that all accountants can agree on – nothing could be further from the truth. Once one has overcome this conceptual obstacle, it then becomes easier to grasp the idea that one must learn how to read between the lines of financial statements, applying financial ratios and externally gained knowledge where possible. Without these skills you cannot spot a bargain.

There is also the need for some broad knowledge of business phenomena. Take, for example, the problem of detecting impending company failure, which is one area that is amenable to ratio analysis.

Studies show that the financial ratios of companies which go bust are markedly different from those which survive and prosper, even five years before they fail. Compared with successful firms in the same industries, failed companies tend to have:

● A low return on capital expended.

● High debt.

● Little cash.

● High accounts receivable.

● Low stock levels.

As the unsuccessful companies approach collapse, the difference between their ratios and those of healthy companies tend to get markedly worse. Here's a table based on a study which illustrates this:

Ratio	Years to failure		
	5	3	1
Cash flow/total debt			
Surviving companies	0.45	0.46	0.45
Failed companies	0.15	0.15	0.15
Total debt/total assets			
Surviving companies	0.37	0.37	0.37
Failed companies	0.51	0.51	0.79
Working capital/total assets			
Surviving companies	0.41	0.41	0.41
Failed companies	0.30	0.30	0.06
Current ratio			
(Current assets/current liabilities)			
Surviving companies	3.4	3.3	3.3
Failed companies	2.5	2.5	2.0
Net income/total assets			
Surviving companies	0.06	0.06	0.06
Failed companies	0.04	0.0	0.2

(Source: Principles of Corporate Finance (McGraw Hill), by R. Brearley and H. Myers)

While the actual figures vary according to country and conditions, the principle is plain: it is possible to spot the signs of failure early, if you know what to look for.

Ratios generally cannot be used blindly; it is essential to ensure that you are comparing like with like. When comparing one company with another which operates in different industries or even different markets, ratios will not usually generate meaningful figures. Although Templeton has said that he relies on secondary information to a large extent – using published calculations of ratios, for example – private investors are probably wise to learn to calculate them for themselves, making adjustments to figures in financial statements in accordance with their knowledge of the company concerned. This is a useful apprenticeship, and one that many young professionals are forced to undergo at the beginning of their careers.

Ratio analysis is best used for:

● Assessing trends within a single company, and

● Comparing companies in similar markets.

Little-understood risks

In the context of bargain hunting, it is worth considering some aspects of risk that are often ignored:

● Environmental risk.

● Competitive risk.

● Equity risk.

Environmental risk

Environmental risk refers to risks to the company arising from external forces, such as the potential impact on the company of government policy, fiscal changes, labour laws and practices, exchange rate practices and policy, environmental (i.e. green) laws and practices.

You should be able to answer questions such as:

● What will happen to your firm or a firm in which you have invested if sterling unexpectedly rises in value against the currency of its main commercial rival?

● What legislation might be on the horizon that could impact on your company – domestically or overseas?

● If the company has a high proportion of part-time employees, what might the potential pension implication cost?

● If it has a large number of low-skilled and low-paid people, what are the implications of a potential minimum wage being imposed?

Competitive risk

Here are some common-sense questions to ask yourself about the company and its competitors:

● Who is gaining market share – and at who's expense?
Think of the enormous price warfare between the major broadsheets.

● How great is the threat from new entrants and what are the barriers to entry?

In a service business the barriers to new entrants will be small – in the bulk chemicals or pharmaceutical businesses barriers include huge investment in research and plants.

● What threats are there from alternative or substitutes to the companies product or service?

IBM, although dominant in the mainframe market, was hit hard not by anybody doing mainframe computers better but because they could not respond quickly enough when customers shifted towards PCs.

● What is the nature of the relationship with suppliers?

● Who dictates the trading terms, and holds the power?

● If a small company is reliant on the output of a huge concern for its business, what does it do when the large company discontinues the production of the material it needs – can it find an alternative source?

● If you find that most of your company's output is purchased by a single large company who has a number of other companies able to supply it with similar goods, how can it resist their demand for a price reduction?

When assessing a company keep asking yourself, 'what if?'. Think of the major relationships between buyers and suppliers in the market – is your company dominant, dependent or in between? Is it a strong player in the market able to influence terms, or an also-ran with a low market share having to accept the prevailing price?

Equity risk

Equity risk means the risk that any investor, including a company, faces is that their portfolio will not perform as well as the general average of the market. A drop in the value of a company's shares can adversely affect its ability to borrow money, and, in some cases, to win large contracts. The variability of the Stock Market as a whole, known as the 'market risk', is different from the variability of individual shares. This great insight forms the basis of the 'Capital Asset Pricing Model' theory (CAPM), beloved of academics but justly regarded with suspicion by many investors.

To compare the movements of a particular share with the Stock Market overall, we say that the 'beta' (the Greek letter 'b') of the market risk is 1. A share with a beta of 2 will swing twice as much as the market does in either direction, and a share with a beta of 1.5 will swing only one and a half times as far. Thus, the higher the beta of a portfolio or individual share, the more risky it is.

'Beta' is a recognised definition of risk, and you can obtain estimates of the beta of a stock from brokers and investment advisers or from published data.

Giving the overall market risk a beta value of 1, and a 'risk-free' investment, such as a bank deposit, a beta value of 0, CAPM uses formulas to work out the expected return on a diversified portfolio.

It's all very neat and internally consistent, but, unfortunately, it appears to be balderdash. Why? Because there is no really sound way of calculating a company's beta. CAPM is useful in so far as it reminds you that a 'bargain' may have a high beta – i.e. it may be considerably more volatile than the market average – but that is as far as it goes. Investment, like making love, is not done well by rote.

– Chapter Four –

On having immaculate judgement

Investment, of course, is not a life-and-death situation, nor should it be. If it is not fun, if it doesn't make you feel good to be alive, then managing your own investments is a waste of time. To this extent, contrarians are born, not made, since the successful ones really do enjoy their occupation. What should be clear, though, is that contrarians come in all shapes and sizes, and bring very different talents to bear on their work, so there is no reason to think that you have to be a genius in order to succeed.

Like great painters, great investors master the basics of their craft before they do their best work. Or, as Vidal Sassoon likes to say, "the only place where success comes before work is in the dictionary". A simple, unpalatable saw, but true nonetheless. You don't have to be sophisticated to become rich, nor do you have to be a crook; motivation and self-knowledge are what really matter.

Contrarians tend to work alone, be hugely knowledgeable in their own area of expertise, and draw on their own natural strengths in choosing their investment approach. Taking the long view helps them to ignore the pressures of the competitive spirit, a cultural phenomenon which is greatly overvalued in our society. They are not trying to be better than anyone else – they are merely trying to make money in the markets.

There is one more factor, though, that they seem to share, even if they deny it – intuition. Intuition is one of those vague ideas that will not yield to rational analysis; it can't be measured or quantified, and it can't be had for the asking.

One can't say, "I am going to make intuitive decisions all day today" with much hope of success. But if, in the course of the day, you suddenly feel a strong certainty that a certain thing will happen to a company, or that you should undertake a particular course of action – act on it.

Twenty years ago an elderly Russian gentleman told me a story which has always stayed with me. A Jew, he was born in St. Petersburg before the revolution, the son of a well-to-do doctor. As a young man he came to England in the late Thirties and tried to make a living as a freelance journalist. At that time his father was working in Danzig (now Gdansk in Poland), a free port into which refugees were pouring, desperate to escape Europe. His father was busy treating sufferers from tuberculosis and other infectious diseases so that they could become eligible for US visas, and was unwilling to leave for England until the last moment. He and his son had an arrangement; if his son, with better access to news in London than his father had in Danzig, thought that war would break out, he was to call his father (inevitably, the lines were tapped) and give the coded message, "It's going to rain".

Life was not easy for the son in England. One day in 1939 he went to Bush House to try to sell a story to the BBC World Service. Unsuccessful, he wandered back towards Trafalgar Square, bought a newspaper and went into a Lyons tea house.

Buried in the middle pages of the paper he saw a tiny snippet of news – 'Herr Hitler has changed the uniform of his personal bodyguard from SS to Wehrmacht (regular army)'. Inspiration hit him, and he telephoned his father to say that it would rain. His father was doubtful; "Are you sure?" he demanded. The son insisted that he was sure. His father took the next boat for England.

For three days nothing happened. His father was furious, especially when he discovered what had prompted his son to call him to London. Then Hitler invaded Poland; the father's boat was the last to leave Danzig.

What immaculate timing!